In a Moment, Poems

by

Jim Stone

Finishing Line Press
Georgetown, Kentucky

In a Moment, Poems

ACKNOWLEDGMENTS

I wish to express my gratitude to the staff of Finishing Line Press, and also
my thanks to Leah Huete de Maines, Publisher and to Christen Kincaid,
Editor for their diligence and devotion to excellence in taking my manuscript
through the publishing process to create the finished book.

Publisher: Leah Huete de Maines
Editor: Christen Kincaid
Cover Art: *Michael's Forest* by Benjamin Stone
Author Photo: Jo Stone
Cover Design: Elizabeth Maines McCleavy

Order online: www.finishinglinepress.com
also available on amazon.com

Author inquiries and mail orders:
Finishing Line Press
PO Box 1626
Georgetown, Kentucky 40324
USA

Table of Contents

I.

Tipping point

I hear it, Dan says. Nothingness is calling, tugging on everything that is.
Fields of grass and forests too are burning everywhere, transforming whole
vistas into ash, free-floating, drifting down.

Ken and his wife, my neighbors, nearly died last summer
in a cabin they had rented every Fourth of July week for over twenty years.
Their holiday neighbors up the road did die
in that fire. The rental cabin is still there, but they won't go back. A raging
night fire is a noisy and troubling visitor.

I wonder at the soft whoosh of movement away to yesterday,
pulling on tomorrow. The sky is losing all its blue to hazy gray-white clouds
and dark smoke. Grit will cover those who go our way and all who follow.

I see it in the morning light, he says, coming from points unseen, bent gray
from blue and almost incandescent; it comes as rays
to molecular nooks, scattering high, falling as music, descending to the next
moment of quiet, creating the next shimmer of gray. Look, only look and
you will see the world is turning away, away from us.

A million birds died last month in summer snow; a million more may die
tomorrow. We are losing plants, elephants, eagles, bees, blue whales, oceans,
wetlands, dry lands and more, but these are only the familiar losses; we
are losing far more than we can know. So much of this world we do not
see or love is dying. Earth doesn't need us; it's we who will vanish with the
eagles and the bees. It's we who caused it, and only we can prevent the full
catastrophe.

I close my eyes, listen for Fall and smell the smoke. Then I hear houses
exploding, destroyed by tornadoes spawned by giant hurricanes that roll
onto our southern coasts
with ever greater frequency.

Look and you too will see whole regions engulfed by floods, millions of
people displaced by the destruction and thousands lost in flood and fire,
whole towns burned to the ground.

People on the street leisurely walk in the hot sun and cooling mist. They
don't notice the destruction or won't.
The mist, like fog, is everywhere.

How Tommy came to be

I was lead navigator on the Mission
to Soong Sai, on a large bomber,
on a large air base, on a small island
where men quietly filed
into the briefing room.
At ten-thirty the major marched in,
pulled the curtain back revealing
the target, twenty-eight hundred
miles distant, and the briefing began.
We can't take out the harbor;
we can't touch the foreign ships,
but every bullet every shell
every article of food must cross
the bridge at Soong Sai.

Lights dimmed;
the screen filled with small photos.
Then each of the small photos was
shown enlarged, full screen,
first the bridge then
the city, the harbor,
the container ships,
the freighters,
the warehouses,
the roads,
and a much clearer, detailed
photo of the bridge at Soong Sai.
This is Soong Sai, he said, raising
his pointer to the bridge at Soong Sai.

Hwei prepared breakfast before dawn.
She and her husband, Ohn, began
eating while their two children slept.
Hundreds of men and women
between the bridge and harbor
began their day in the same fashion.

Ohn gently shook Mahti, his son.
Time to feed the chickens, he said.
Then he picked up the day-bag Hwei
had packed and pedaled off toward
the warehouses near the harbor.

Once there he greeted his friends
and exchanged his empty bicycle
for another, heavy with many bags,
small sacks, and steel tools.
Balancing the unwieldy bicycle
(he didn't ride it), he pushed off
with hundreds of others
toward the bridge.

The morning sun broke
through the low clouds
as Ohn crossed the bridge,
and the gray dawn faded
to brilliant green and gold.
From the bridge he could

see for miles. His world was
warm, shining, beautiful.
In that beauty the jungle was
less formidable, looming ahead.
Ohn smiled thinking of Hwei
and their happy children.

He was deep in the jungle on
the narrow trail when the first
explosion ripped the day.
Far out of range, he didn't hear it.
It seemed to distant eyes as if
many small, white clouds instantly

and silently appeared from nowhere
on the bridge and around it.
There were clouds in the village, too.
The village was consumed. His small
house, his beautiful wife and children,
even his chickens were gone.

A coming storm

dwarfs Midge and Dan's small house. It's even
smaller among the surrounding fields. The sun
sinks behind the barn; soon the yard light comes on
flooding the shadows and closing the day like a
goodnight kiss. Scattered stars hide the edge of the
storm; they dim and fade then disappear. Soon
the night is dark, black as a miner's nightmare.

Crickets turn on and quickly turn off. The wind
kicks up and hurls a box across the yard. Quick
as it came, the wind dies down. The moon and
night's strange shapes are gone. A stronger wind
and colder now fills the air with dirt and straw,
blows it around the yard striking the screens
like a hard rain pounding the roof.

Midge turns out the light, climbs into bed
and says, Goodnight, Love—Is it raining?
Not yet but smells like rain, Dan answers
as he closes the window.
Sleep comes in with the dark.

Bam!   A box strikes the house.

Dan's up like a shot, still groggy. Midge sits up, hears Dan
talking to Jack, who follows him through the door. Stay there,
Honey, Dan shouts, I'm waiting for Wally. I'll get them
sonsabitches yet. He sits and fingers the rifle across his lap.
She dozes for two or three hours. *Damn that Wally*, she whispers
and tip-toes to the front room where man and, dog snore.

*Wally's dead, Dan. It's the ghosts you brought home from the
war,* she whispers and touches his arm. He startles, she kisses
his cheek, *shhh*, she says, helps him up and takes the gun,
leads him back to bed, then checks the gun empty and leans it
against the wall behind the door.

Midge worries about Dan and Wally, the invisible men in his head
who trouble the night. Wally also troubles the day as it loses its light
while she's constantly thinking, 'We're really not safe. Careful. Wake
him gently. Don't startle him with alarm. Don't think about Wally, not
living not dead.'

Soliloquy on suicide

Dan sips his scotch as he speaks to the empty
room and the darkness beyond the walls.

I go on because that's what there is,
a few days then another storm, another
trip through the crusher mill that would
squeeze the last drop of me from me.

Who can know you? Nils dared not try.
He knew the dark, secret smile of deception,
and how well did he know fear. He found it
in ██████████ after landing at ██████████
We all did. (Nils gathered it in like
a blanket around him.) Why we were sent
to and stationed in ████████████████ ██████████
who can say? Once there we were on patrol
and in several engagements. We lost ██████████
of ours, ██████████ in ██████████ and
on patrol
in the first month.

We gathered their personal effects to send home
and burned the bloody gear that was left. Fear
became the thing. It isolated many and drove
out all warmth, all light with bleak
and unwavering doubt, hopeless doubt.

Fear and terror played with us. There was no
comforter and no faith for Nils. It was a casualty
of combat, of death all around, the death of
friends we came in with, trained with and lost.
There was no peace for Nils. He seemed always
on edge, possessed by isolation, anxiety and fear,
but he was affected or showed it more than
the rest of us.

Faith is a weakness, he said, a feather to hold
for those afraid. I knew Nils.
He didn't know you. You, Silence, who could?
Nils and I were discharged together, went home
and started college. He was married; I lived in the dorm.

It appeared we were fine during the first six months,
and then his wife called and asked me to find Nils.

I recall the dark, the rain and the bridge abutment. I remember too,
the bright lights flying passed, the tires of those speeding cars and
trucks screaming by and the flashing red, blue, white and yellow
lights of police cars, fire engines, ambulance and the scattered
debris.

His car was shattered, dark, reflecting no light.
Suicide, the officer said.

It's not like he fought back. He seemed to
prefer despair. Like his drunken father's,
his world was black. Blame it on combat,
the war, medication—blame it on college,
his wife.

You, your silence, there is no blame for you.
That last night, he despaired and pulled
darkness up tight to cover fear and end thought.
Few noticed or cared. Few ever do, but his friends
cared; I cared, though nothing we did helped.
Perhaps you blame it on Nils.

But you left us, all of us, on that hill; Nils, Dirk,
Frankie, all the others and I scattered around,
refusing to run, even to move, giving our all
to repel Wally, still probing, gunning for us.
You weren't finished even then; you brought
us here, brought us home still anxious, uneasy,
clearing the field, gunning for ghosts.

Soldier of moments,

Dan witnessed but did not see
Phillips flying wing and Vice lead
on a ground support mission—two
thousand marines pinned down by
thirty-five-hundred enemy at the border
and in their SAM zone.

Heavier at three g's, Phillips strains to keep
his eyes on the target. The aircraft continues
climbing as earth rolls beneath blue sky
and moves across the canopy while the craft
rotates and floats inverted hung on blue;
Phillips floats there too looking up at earth
and his target.

In that space and time, floating inverted,
mind splits as it sometimes does. He's home
to see his beautiful wife, his boy and his
toddling girl standing in the front yard
waving as he had seen them on takeoff when
the entire wing with its three squadrons left
family and home for war.

He sees his children and pregnant wife;
he misses them, longs to hold them close again
in that flack-troubled moment above the target.
"I love you," he says softly as the aircraft rolls
out on the bomb run, passing seven thousand
feet and descending.

He pictures his little boy laughing, running
and stumbling in the soft dirt of the recently
plowed field behind his house as he centers
the target in the bomb sight and airspeed
passes five-hundred knots.

Then it happens, that once-in-a-million shot;
he freezes in the descent, out of breath, in
shock and mumbles, "Pickle," as he releases
the bombs. The aircraft hits the ground beyond
the target, beyond explosions, life and light.

Nightshift at Dan's first job

The long shift ends at two as people
line up to punch the clock and gather
their things for the bus ride home.

Goodnights are said, then quiet comes on.
Thought is the only voice that's heard until
the squeal of brakes as the bus pulls up.

Cool air slides into shadows telling the
crickets the night is young.

They have their music and play their song
for the nightshift march to the bus ride home.

Inside the bus it's bright as day; it never
dims no matter how late or loud the song.

Motion slows as shops close. Tired women
and tired men come from all around.

Some wave for the last bus home to wait
then rush toward the engine whine.

Tires hum. The tired sleep on. Heads bob
and nod as the bus bumps along.

I-70, west

from Burlington, sharing the driving with Tommy—
much of the afternoon we've watched mountains rise
from the horizon to a low, faint and misty blue shadow
then to the massif before us and beside.

We passed the turnoff to Grays and Torreys Peaks trailhead
on the left a few miles back. Now there's no summit in sight,
nothing but highway, mountain and forest.

Up the steep slope to the right, a large grove of trees shines
bright yellow with a touch of pink to red among the tall pine.
Aspen leaves play in the sunlight and flash, quaking
in the breeze.

We've been driving hard since Kansas City. Now at last we've
pulled off the highway into a 'scenic view'. We plan to rest,
sleep if we can.

In the shadows of night on that slope, trees seem like people.
The whole grove sways with the wind, silently watches stars
turn as shadows change and lengthen while the moon sails
through the night spreading silver as it goes.

They remember nothing of what they were, know nothing of
what they are, a sacred grove of those lost, missing, missed,
merely gone and sought. They stand where they've stood for
years, leaning from the wind and swaying day and night;

they talk as trees to all trees on the mountain through a network
of roots, but they sing in the wind to the wind, to each other,
to the pine covering the rest of the mountain, to the mountain,
to all mountains and to us. They do not commune with nature;
they are part of it. They do not feel the pulse of Earth because
they are part of that pulse. They are brought by the wind;
the moving air we breathe and live by brings them.
They are as numerous as trees because they are…

At two-twenty-two A.M. I'm barely conscious;
we're moving up the mountain from the scenic view.
Sorry, Restless Tommy says, didn't mean to wake you. I woke,
couldn't get back to sleep, thought I might as well be driving.
There's a tunnel ahead; it's one we'll be going through.

Gene about his neighbor, Clete

He takes the shade all summer,
hardly looks up, hasn't
in forty years, Gene tells us.

He walks across the yard,
ball-cap on, head down, mumbling,
kicking the dry leaves.

Time for the damned ole rake,
he says to no one, rake
the god-damned leaves.

At dusk he tiredly stows
the rake, the last leaf finally
sacked and stacks the sacks

by the sidewalk near the street.
Silently during the night,
the grand old cottonwood

appears to smile as it
drops another twenty
bushels neatly, everywhere.

II

Daffodil Sun

I had a dream, Tommy says
to Gene, only casually listening,
thinking of Tommy and his place.
The sun came out. Daffodils by
the hundreds exploded on an
isolated hillside in our town.
The bright blue sky, green grass
and yellow flowers went unseen
from the street by the thousands
speeding toward an anxious day
in cubicles and meetings. They
may realize at the fading

light and last echo of their being
this shimmering, shining daffodil sun
could have been theirs, was in fact theirs.
They looked at it; they knew of it. But
they missed it. For a sum of money, for
a fifteen room museum, they missed it.
They traded it for game shows, Friday
night fights over phantom income,
house payments and endless bills.

For a fast train to nowhere, the chance
to curry favor from one more poisonous
toad, they missed their moment and its
beauty. Some call me Homeless Tommy
because I live here in a refrigerator box
hidden in a large Chinese juniper grove.
I move freely among the daffodils of
the park; I own nothing but cast-offs,
a few blankets and utensils I found
dumpster-diving.

In the scale of the city, the scale of
plenty, of never enough, of more and
more, screw the poor, the scale
of surviving, of scheming, driving,
screaming and crying, of dying with
no reason to live, I am no one. I am
nothing.

Every day bliss is found in what you
give away, I said that, and I know
the magnificence of each day's dawn,
the chill of morning, and occasional
smiles on the jogging path, that's all I
own. It's free and I share what I can,
for I am a wealthy man.

At that, Gene bent down, cut two flowers
and stood smiling as he gave a daffodil
to Tommy, his cousin, and carried
the other like a prize to his old Plymouth.
He got in and sputtered off.

Later a letter came from the city citing
Code Section 1789.

"We have information from
a witness willing to testify
that on the above date you
were picking flowers in the
greenbelt, a violation of
Code Section 1789

"Fine $65.00.

"Please return payment in
the enclosed envelope.
Unstamped replies will be
returned. The yellow copy
is for your records."

Ah, Tommy.
Tommy, you turned me in.

From hard days to empty nights

Gene looked up
from the stack
of papers in his hand
and smiled, faintly.
I don't know that
you know, he said,
my wife and I
are separated.

He paused and looked away.
It's been a hard time.
Not like I'm surprised,
but I thought—
I thought—
I'd hoped we could keep it
together.

It's a sorry ending
to twenty-eight years.
He looked away again.
His lip trembled.

I moved out last week,
Found a little apartment
not far from here.
I'd hoped we could
keep it together.
But that's our world,
our time. Everything
changes so fast, even people.

He paused, looked out the
window and stared
at the mountains, cirrostratus
hung high there horizon to
horizon, north to south
along the front range.
He turned again
to his papers
and walked
away midsentence.

Calendar day

for Gene who looks first
at December's photograph.
Gene has changed jobs.
He stares vacantly at the July
picture, an ancient tower
in China built years ago,

thirteen hundred, in fact.
Crows circle above.
He's heavier now, his face
jowly as if age is pulling,
weighing him down.
It's beer and age.

That's my fate, he tells
Tommy. His hair is no
longer cut too short or
bright yellow laced with
orange mixed with brown.
I can be Mr. Corporate, he says.

He changed it for interviews
and works at the bank now;
days pass in isolation on
the fourth floor drafting
trusts, dreaming trusts,
and reviewing trusts.

The law firm let him go
after he and Jack got in a
tussle, their version.
His description, the best
day of my life. I knocked

Jack on his ass like I did playing
high school football, only just as
Mr. Collins, senior partner, firm
manager and Jack's father, came
out of his office. I lost that job.

Glowing buildings stand tall in
December's early morning dark.
The blowing cold chills his ears
and numbs his cheeks as he
crunches through the snow,

his breath a cloud of muted rainbow.
Smiling at the nameplate on the door,
404 - File and Storage, he enters
and lights come on as he remembers
the disconcerted Mr. Collins.

He smiles again, at stepping over Jack,
as he sets his brief case on his desk
and briefly relives his exit interview.
Not working out, *not working out?*

The computer whines, tick, glance
at the clock; he stares at his calendar,
December's photograph, a tower,
a murder of crows circles against a
snowy mountain.

Another day—making toast

It's dawn, the time of day you'll find me sitting
by the front window in the rocker watching for
the sun and the living. No sun today, but I sit here
slowly rocking, thinking and looking out the window
at the cold winter wind ripping across the empty,
barren and seemingly lifeless landscape.

I look for the tenacious creatures that live here,
the struggling and tenuous life that bears the assault
and suffers through the difficulties to warm
and pleasant days.

I watch the white wilderness. It's like a desert,
only white and frozen. Its inhabitants wake up
to the light, the day and the fulfilment of an old
promise. A solitary crow lands on my feeder with
a nod my direction, just as I see it, and immediately
pecks at the large ball of suet and nuts.
She's a frequent guest, returns several times a day,
occasionally with the whole family, but mostly alone.
We've become acquainted; I call him (or her) Bill.
Bill calls to the others, and they sometimes come
one by one, warily.

No wind now, mostly calm, gentle as a baby's
breath. The yard light turns off, but I can still see
the gray sky dropping feathers. Falling feathers look
like snow; they cover the spruce and gently follow
the slightest breeze or strike like hail when hard
winds blow. There's a puzzling shape in white
and tan down by the gate; no movement there,
then a quick leap with immeasurable ease changes
the view to a doe with her fawn stuck under the fence.

Wiggling free, it's unimpressed by her effortless flight on
invisible wings. It's a moment of quiet, no worries awake;
it's too early to shovel and too cold to check.

Here's Jack—usually comes in with the coffee and Midge. He always wants out. I asked Midge if she also wanted out, teasing her. She always declined, but this time she said she would think about it. Then she was off to make the toast, she said. But three days ago? Went to town…?

Recitation from the street

Gene, I used this little recitation to ask for money when I was living on
the street. It echoed my feelings about who and where I'd been,
trying get home. Gil and Dan backed me up. Gil on guitar,
Dan on harmonica.

> been a long time gone
> long time coming back
> loving you is all there is of me
>
> nearly died in a distant fight
> nearly drowned in whiskey nights
> loving you is all there is
>
> went to war but marched for peace
> sang Jesus songs till explosions ceased
> loving you is all there is of me
>
> been broken up and spat upon
> burnt black in jail by an angry man
> loving you is all there is
>
> at the edge of life beyond this town
> you helped me up steadied my ground
> loving you is all there is
>
> loving you is all there is of me
> loving you is all there is.
>
> Any change,
> any spare change you could share?
> God bless you anyway, bless you.
>
> Thank you.
> God bless you, bless you.

We also sang a few songs. I tapped the bongos as Gil strummed
and picked. Dan blew a wild harmonica, but when he sang,
Dan just rattled. We met in jail, drunk-tank, I think.
We split the bread.
Be in touch.
    Tommy

Tommy variations

1.   With consideration—I sometimes am afraid;
            I fear the darkness fear the night.

            I hear the music in my head
            and hear the moments' tinnitus
            whispering eternal sighs.

            Light moves very fast, more quickly
            than the dash of hands and feet or
            coming dawn; it flashes passed the
            tumbling river and the river's song.

            I am afraid of blight, of love withering away
            to ultimate decay and the destruction of bright
            sunshine days. I go alone, often lose my way,
            and I am lost, frightened still wondering.

            I hear people cry, feel their sorrow,
            their murmur, their moan. Listen,
            can you hear the cello playing?
            It's the music of earth and sky.

            Though unacquainted, we travel together,
            you and I, through our separate selves,
            and this rhyme, knowing day fades as
            we do from our common space and time.

2.   Tomorrow will come again
            until it fails to dawn, and I
            no longer am the foolish one
            who fears the absent light.

            Silence envelopes me
            and all I am or hoped to be.
            Darkness holds tight
            and will not let go.

There is a darkness at the edge
of light pushing and pushing
toward the night, and I can't open
my eyes; I can't begin to see.

Everything collapses into—nothingness,
and I can't find the door.
There's no remembering where
it was, no remembering at all.

It seems a symphony streaming in black,
but there's no sound where sound
is never coming back—a troubling
dream, formless and undefined.

3.   There is that infinite… what?
something? The great and vast
complexity that is and was before
before and will be after I am not

silence quite, not emptiness or
naught because the door no
longer swings and sound is
not where nothing sings.

No light, no dark, not even
thought except the one that
is the one that makes it all
and ends it all and then
begins again where light
is neither light nor dark, where
time no longer tics or tocks.

Why am I here?
I sometimes ask myself
this question, knowing the answer.
A diamond scratches it clearly
on the window of my mind,
retracing it daily.
"I will to be, I must be
here," it reads, then not.

4.   Where once and only once we
were and once and only once

we are, there never was or will
be another you or I.

There's no begin, begin again
or take it from the top. The top

was once as we were then;
there is no more begin again.

Specificity does not increase the fact:
there is an only once, a last and final act.

Sometimes we see as others see, stepping
over friends that used to be or flying by.

We feel as Nils that dreadful pull. It will not
heal but kills, wind whispers in a languid sigh.

5.   My thoughts of you continue
like drifting moments   moving through
the milky blue   beyond the lace
of trees and time.

I see you
thinking, wondering in a stalled lane
and staring ahead, mulling over
tomorrow's list, considering the who
and what tomorrow brings.

The little things we carry are
different from the ancients' load,
though we are much the same as
they in changing light at end of day.

The sun slides by the shadowed hills;
behind them larger darkness looms,
created by high mountains and cold night,
pushing out the afterglow, and then
it's just the happy sight of you.

6.   You touch me.
        I would dance   with you forever.

        You kiss me   and I am filled
        with joy as we spin.

        We embrace and hold
        each other tight   dancing down the line.

        The crowded room   grows even more fantastic
        as we spin   and turn and then we spin again.

        Turning, we have come   full circle round
        and laugh   in the glowing night.

        It's dark and cold and we laugh some more
        and turn and spin   then we go 'round again

7.   Words burn when spit in hate or anger
        and stun like water from a frozen lake;
        words can be the soothing drink that calms
        a pounding heart and lets the drinker think.

        Words can be the frozen lies hurled
        through time and space to cut,
        to skewer, to twist and steal
        an injured soul from grace.

        The wounded will not be smiling soon
        when words have done their trick.
        They cut inside and burn like pride
        till every breath is nicked.

Yet words are mute if we but close the door
and find the light that is and was before before.

8.   Do we only listen
to the music
we were given by the stars,
or do we sing?

Sometimes in the darkness
beneath the cloudy night,
I hear the music flowing—voices singing

faintly on a breeze, a high soprano
sounding out   the sorrows of the age,
a distant tenor   pleading for the day.
The darkness feels so heavy yet

weighs nothing more than light.
We gather as we do to bring our warmth
and strength against our fears.
They are the many and we the few.

9.   This April morning burns through dawn
as life stirs.

How it goes: we want to mean, have a touch
of permanence, significance beyond the flowers,
tulips dancing with the wind or rose bouquets.
Call it self-indulgence; it is without a doubt.

I've come to wait with my sister.
I see her sitting motionless, eyes closed, across
the quiet hall, a giant room.
The nurse called it Reception Hall though it's
less hall than auditorium.

A nurse approaches, they talk; a clock drops,
someone shouts, I turn to see and turn back
again to find both gone, the moment passed.

End of summer, last prayer of Autumn, skies
turn orange then red, turn pink then black;
I sensed her fear as we came across town.
Words require thought; keeping her
composure took all her energy; we
did not speak. Now she's faint
and bleeding, in much pain.

The nurse waves to beckon me;
I follow him and find her weak—
her body frail, her mind a fog.

She wanders confused
among the flowers,
dreaming,
in anguish still.

The world is diminished and days bleak
when one so loved is suddenly gone.
Words stumble in the shadows of grief
and the sorrows of loss.

As day closes, flowers burn
in the light and heat of murmuring flames—

10.   Night comes to cover us,
cover our moment.
The father, the mother,
a puzzle, the mystery
confuses and troubles
the daughters, the sons.
Each, a bewildering perplexity,
confounds the others
and the father, the mother
who wonder and wonder.

We find them in shadows
and bring them into light
only to find more shadows,
shadows of the mind, images
in time we cannot touch,
cannot know, but see them,
hear them like the wind blowing
through the trees of dreams,
pushing on the branches, scraping
on the walls, moving slowly like
the tide moves, out to sea again.

Jim **Stone** graduated from the University of Colorado-Boulder where he studied Mathematics and the physical sciences. While at college, he also worked on the student literary magazine with his wife, Jo Stone, who was the editor, and together they also worked on *Penny Poetry*.

After graduating, he went into the Air Force, graduated from pilot training, and flew a fighter. He was pursuing the dream of becoming an astronaut, and failing that, cut short his Air Force service after five years. He and his wife then started a child care center with funds they saved in the Air Force and other funds they gathered from squadron friends and family. The business was later sold, and the proceeds divided among investors.

After several years in financial services James joined The College for Financial Planning where he wrote and taught the course, Retirement Planning and Employee Benefits and taught the Investment Planning course for the University of Phoenix.

Today, Jim and Jo have been happily married longer than Christmas and have four grown children. Jo still manages her law firm and meets with clients while James reads, writes, revises and writes some more.